مف OPH

TANIA KHALIL

First edition, Turning Point Books, 2022

Text copyright © Tania Khalil, 2022
Layout and graphic design copyright © Turning Point, 2022

Front cover design by Hamza Mekdad
Inside layout by Miriam Fayad

Printing by 53 Dots
ISBN 978-9953-972-25-1
All rights reserved.

No part of this publication may be reproduced or submitted in any form or any means without the written permission of the author.

with love, to my mother

special thanks to
miriam fayad, jameel dabbagh, and hamza mekdad
in art, friendship is eternal

table of contents

7	intro
9	twenty-seven
11	stalling
13	damn it
15	stuffed animals
17	potential
19	twelve
21	i am a girl
23	display
25	curtain call
27	temporary
29	a while
31	a feeling
33	small
35	i conduct the fire
37	poetic divide
39	stay with me
41	christina's world
43	chosen
47	almost

49	muse
51	the last doll
53	mm-eh
55	pen me down
57	restroom
59	thirty-two
61	radish rose
63	bloom
65	noise
67	modern spree
69	the taste of love
71	those too
73	the morning after
75	freetown
77	key rose
79	float
81	inherited madness
83	a room outside
85	outro

intro

thread yourself together
in circular motions
on white cloth
:
the long hours
sober and hard to stand
may be worth it

twenty-seven

the lampshade light is flickering
revealing the outline of a naked fly, gasping
for air
a gentle reminder that life is strange and undying
it was hard, i know
you're sorry, i know
home videos are playing in my mind and i'm thinking
why?

:

the red pill melts like hot molasses under my tongue
a single drop of red dye now spreading inside my body
generously hazing over everything
like leafless stems of climbing roses
taking over
i am not a pill taker
but that night

:

the phone rings
he's gone

:

happy pills kicking in
happy pills
twice
i try to smile and manage to feel fine
we all leave this planet when it's time

:

the black mountains under my eyes have settled on my skin
and the grapes
they don't taste the same
their violet now feeds my bruises
my breath is heavy and hardened
i keep telling myself that death will come to the dying
that you just couldn't see the light

:

allow me
i am a luminous animal guarding the black sand castle that awaits you
from a wave determined to wash you away
rest in peace against my hand
and sleep
i will wake you up when we arrive
and spread angel bait around your crystal eyes

stalling

i am nine years of age
waiting for supper to be served
in the living room of house number four
where we no longer live
:
the kitchen cabinet creaks
an indication the cereal box is back in place
powdered milk is on it's way
flakes soak in anticipation of my halvah heat
absent from the body that carries me and alive in every form of mischief
i find myself moaning in a playground of man-made peace
the door creaks
uh oh
i play it cool and change the channel
still oblivious to why my cruel intentions need parental guidance
as if a full movie is enough to describe the tender trouble at hand

damn it

the dust prances around me in sonic waves
like fireflies moved by a gray wind
concealing their light to fit in
destroyed silver
reduced to familiar ashes
giving rise to an abandoned ocean inside
:
knock knock
anyone there?
scratch
knock knock
anyone care?
scratch
knock knock
it is i father i swear!
scratch
knock knock
i am bare!
scratch
the black telephone's off at the root
it's me dad
i'm here for dinner
scratch
another wound another door
the time for growth is now

stuffed animals

i did not flinch when he turned me around
both hands pressing down
a giant handprint from art class
slapped like a wet sticker on my behind
two hands
he moves
his chest persuades my small back to stay put
cotton caresses my right cheek
grape-less young goddess that is me
i did not flinch
:
stuffed animals
sheep-like and happy to serve
descend over me like cotton clouds from a kind continent
faraway as childhood
i think of the warm water that awaits me
the paint wears off
the pain is casual
:
afloat in my pink pool
i sink underwater out of sight
grape-less and gulping
for a while
but something inside
pulls me up
and clenches onto the side of the bathtub

potential

doctor
am i a freak?
postpubescent possibilities penetrate my mind
shall i end it
i could
starve myself from the sun
i have
slit my skin like a reckless teen
paint my hair with hair mascara
wash off the black
replace it with pink dye
dead
not this time
it's something a hair perm can't fix
it's deep
i'm self-destructive but sweet
will hurt me but won't hurt you
no one sees
doctor!
sanity is a matter of degrees, sweets
doctor?
you'll be okay
my mother clung to these words like a life raft

twelve

your nipples flashed underneath your shirt early on
you were a curious kid
things excited you
the road less taken
the unknown

i am a girl

i am a girl
i am a tribe
hunting for the angels
that hide where i reside
show me the way
lead me astray
i will pray for my heart to stay forever this way
:
i can't promise you sweet nothings
i am trouble i am soul
my fair lady, not so fair
hold that thought then throw it away
into the wild
i won't bribe you to bride

display

you lie behind a glass window
priced, polished
probing the man in the pale blue penthouse
to rescue you
consumed with answers on silver platters
answers to no questions asked
:
a familiar acquaintance
i met you slowly
then all at once
bleeding rose water on black paper trails
i knew you weren't from here
:
the bluebirds await to dwell in your peaceful resistance
and the house in the hills is alive in anticipation of your arrival
alone
and in love

curtain call

curtains begin to close slowly on me
not any kind of curtains
black lace
a very fine lace
made with black thread and intricate patterns of secret gardens
black roses woven into black gardenias interlaced with black lavender leaves
unusual for theatrical drapery
a curtain call carefully crafted with jarring notions of some other place
some other time
closing on me like a *mimosa pudica*
the shy and shrinking plant that closes on itself
when touched or shaken
defending itself from harm
only to reopen a few minutes later

:

i lie on the floor
arms and legs extended like a tortured prophetess
falling inwards as my spine extends further into the ground and pulls me back
to my earliest memory
like a young woman aging in reverse
further down
initiation stages of a young girl
running back to the place i dreamt of running away from
to see if anyone would notice
i open my eyes
staring at a ceiling of carved scars
pale pink petals separated by thin air
my spine is the trunk of a transparent glass rose
each thorn, a scar of mine
ready to pounce and protect
like a virgin valkyrie ready for battle

temporary

silver pole
star of the silent screen
casting spells in motel rooms
she shines
half naked under her pink wig
short bobs and bangs
in search of an illustrated home
:
a victim of circumstance
this is not her intended dance
to nurture the unloved
pretend to want the unwanted
men in black beg on her nocturnal front door
only to call her a whore in broad daylight
:
fishnets and full of love
her misfortunes will stand in front of their courts
the judge will tremble at her sight
unable to comprehend how her borrowed bed
is more *home*
than their mansions of closed doors

a while

i haven't written in a while
a while can last a lifetime if you let it
i let it
and whilst the while lasted in every breath of revelation
i realized that i was alone with myself
alone with everyone else too
:
now here i am
a so-called grownup
pretending the growth is real
when time itself ran out of time to heal the deep oceans
trapped inside my next door neighbor's swimming pool
as if the doors are even real
:
'i came i saw i conquered'
the national anthem of my generation
inked under ribs, on lower backs
and the bruised senses of self
are blown away
on lines of instant gratification

a feeling

i breathe out the heaviness of breathing in
feels like i've never felt anything before
not numb, just never
:
an hourglass gradually fills me up
fills me in
on the theory
of everything
the plant and the planet
the bird and the plane
the kingdom of ants and the kingdom of god
cross-legged cross-eyed
before my time is up
:
swamped by the science of stillness
my stagnation, a revelation
the gods are burning inside
the men, beside
:
the landscape is changing
yet i remain the same
sand dunes to wild rainforests
the smell of the earth after the rain
in my nostrils
i inhale
the mother takes over
i vanish into that soft dark womb of warmth
the black dog disappears
i have arrived

small

subway symphonies sound like my sense of self
underrated underground
small but brilliant
like the lives of many women

i conduct the fire

i am a restless firefall
a firefall in which burning hot embers
are spilled from the top of a glacier point
to a valley 3,000 feet below
for spectators down under to witness the show.
dug my own grave
hoping to be saved
but the prophets are busy
and i'm on hold to heaven

poetic divide

it's dark outside
inside too
i sit in stillness
stranded
in the river beneath the river
an urge to write about the world
to preserve it in words far less transcending than the simple sensation
of water on water
water on a rock
water on my hands
:
the beauty of this thing i can't describe is too much to bear
what else can i do but replenish from the grace of god
a terminal fraud?
who cares
i write to endure
i write to thrive
:
the ground underneath muffles the sound of my footsteps
a force pulling man and matter together
memento
momentum
it is my time but i don't seem to care

stay with me

i was going to end it
my plan was to invite everyone for a film screening
in my garden
where flowers grow under fairy lights
to celebrate the last day of my life
a kind of beauty that divides itself
between excessive love
and hopelessness
:
stick around, begs my higher self
astronauts carry pills in case they are unable to return to planet earth
you are here this is home
have a carrot, some blueberries
boost the serotonin in your brain
the damage is done, i whisper
not nearly, it whispers back

christina's world

a young woman crawls across a field
toward a small brave house
on top of a hill
the landscape is barren
the lack of color, necessary
in every direction, 500 miles of nothing
she stares into the distance at the prospect of her world

chosen

i have been chosen to consciously deactivate the left side of my brain
a stroke of right side insight supported by the arts council
to withdraw from a place of exaggerated sanity and
extroverted stop signs of
sacred silence
into a world without words
where splitting the second is the only way to navigate through the poetry of
predisposed pain
not the pain in poetry
but the poetry of pain
:
the time is now
i am losing consciousness as i speak
how much of this process is voluntary on the part of the speaker
doesn't necessarily come across
right now
they said i would start referring to myself in the third person
i can see that
it is in my nature to prove them wrong
but my eyes are busy adjusting to a sense of self outside
of me
i'm not sure she'll rebel
but i can try
she means i
(giggles)
i mean i
they are recording my giggles!
wooaw! did you
see
did you see that?
there's an uncontrollable growth of color in the brain room
metallic thorns arranged at equal intervals along the strands of steel
surrounding me
seem to have flattened
into a silver lining
scattered thorns sinking into a cardiac flatline
something in the nature of thorns simply can't survive on silver linings
thorn after thorn
metal collapsing into shimmering silver specks in the space between
steel and stage
thorn after thorn
silver specks slow dancing to a cosmic symphony towards the earth

towards the stage
falling
like a speckled silver halo
flat on the floor in a perfect salt circle
circle of sacred space
continuous, complete
and *mine*
oh, ancient salt circle of protection!
keep me inside your ring of salt
keep me inside
your womb
i don't want to come out

:

wish someone was here
to see
to see how
thorns can disappear
how the world can surprise you with it's grace
to see
wait
they haven't
they haven't disappeared
it's me
it's all me
the thorns appear to have faded
because i have been spinning
am spinning
slowly spinning
turning in my place like an old ceiling fan in a glass castle
stretched out both arms like a delusional dervish under the black brilliant sky
wait
not sky
ceiling
under the black brilliant ceiling
it's all in my head
i see

:

i hear the bluebirds chirping around the wires of my mind
piew piew prude
piew piew
prude
piew
prude
if you were to stop spinning the thorns would appear once again like sad things
do sometimes

something in the nature of sad things just keeps coming back
creeping up on you like cats do before they pounce
and if you're lucky
pounce but also protect

my thoughts are changing
and
i should stop spinning
stop
stopping
need a point of focus
i stare at the window frame hanging on the wall behind me
window frame on wall?
i wonder why it's there
or what it would be like if only i could go outside
and out the other side
of the wall
how do you get out though? and in
in and out
what defines their limit?
these places
outside that door is a hallway
that leads to
another door that leads to
the door that takes you to
the garden
the garden ends and the street is there
and you walk to
no you walk down
the street
to get to your front
door
into your house
through the living room and
into your bedroom
you look out the window
a different window but still a window
can you see the self you left behind?
looking at the prospect of you from where you are now?
it's all starting to feel like one big playground planet place to me

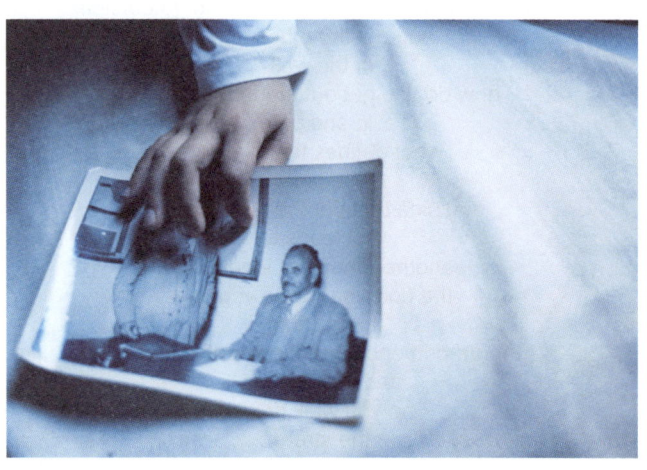

almost

i feel as though somebody's watching me
not watching *over me*
watching *me*
grinding their teeth at my sight
both in pleasure and in spite
like they might

muse

black turtleneck
lacks iron, losing sleep
eyes intending without expecting
looks away from me like it's the sensible thing to do
crosses her arms and caresses herself like she's done this before
doesn't rock, just holds
protective of what's inside
she sighs
slowly tilts her head up to eye level, still looking away
half gazing at the twisted strands of steel skirting the stage
a stage from which all props and pretenses have been removed
everything is painted black including the floor
nothing but naked walls
and her black turtleneck

the last doll

there, there
my wooden doll
bright-eyed and blind
dragging your mother's clothes
let me open you up
spread you on my marble
for guests to see, i've traveled east
:
there, there
my nesting doll, my handmade hen
let me open you up
spread your sisters behind you
like breadcrumbs decreasing in size
my downsize dolls
domesticated
on my marble
:
there, there
my little matron, my last crumb
smallest of them all
sweet and sealed
there is no opening you up
little rose
even your mother would fit in one of my hands

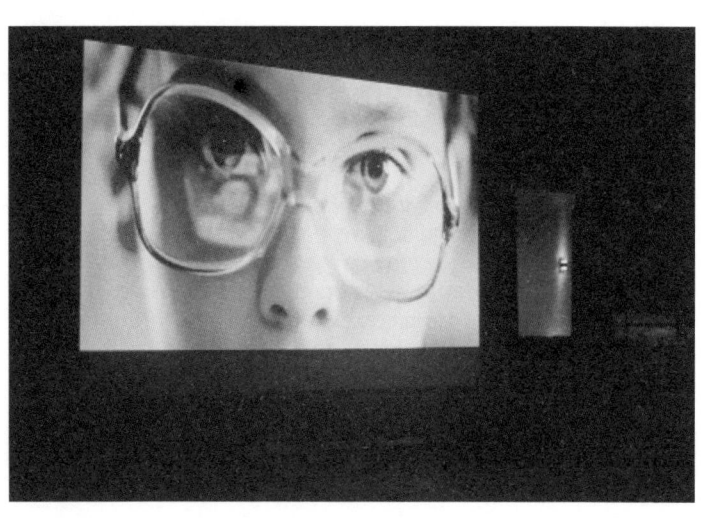

mm-eh

he lies there
fantasizing about the back of my hair
poor kid wouldn't dare
he looks up instead of straight ahead
pretends his conscience is bigger than the size of his
(insert synonym) slant
i stare back
spitting image of a bohemian trying hard to get off track
a victim of nothingness, he remains intact
sweet tooth turns sour
starved soul famished for more
distracted by a dream where i played whore
his world must've been a bore

INVOICE (2)

64

3½ Diet Pepsi   9,000
1 Almaza   5,000

2 meals   ????
             PAY WHAT YOU
             THINK IS FAY

pen me down

the pen won't stop
compelling my soul to sink
sink in pitch black ink
stares at me in spite of me
a crowd of two
a girl and a gun
alphabet armor

restroom

shit-faced among pale pink walls
queen of the awkward foot standing
still if i could
risking disapprovals
involved in my detachment
let go let go
indifferent (lies)
i don't care (lies)
pretending to put off the world

thirty-two

joint close to my chest
high on all kinds of heights
contemplating a passage on emotional intelligence
i start to weep at my last elevator encounter
i wanted to write and he was a writer
thirty-two years apart, thirty-two floors to go
little did i know, there was a lot i didn't know
:
he was older but not wiser
ocean sailing to my dot com generation
he wrote me a love letter and attached a discount price to his paradise
i wrote back and said
'you are everything i hate about exaggerated sanity'
and you don't have to get it

radish rose

delicately carved radish, made to look like a rose
he placed you in ice water overnight
to open you up
petals pulsating outwards in slow motion
pulp
pause
pulp
:
careful with his knife
he peels off the white
and continues all the way across
carving you into being
like one of his classics

:
pulp
pause
pulp
:
he's gone
it's me
hurry up and listen
the dancing force always struggles upwards
so struggle
but struggle upwards
:
release your stoic soul
from the box
of the beloved
you belong in the amazon
where the soil is pure and the sun awaits
begging you to bloom

bloom

my paradise was never a white garden of cashmere walls
and floating harps
rather
i float
endlessly
between the flames of heaven and skies of hell
a place where every pebble is a precious stone
and flowers bloom prematurely
images romanticized to a painful state of closeness
immersed in the warmth my heart tries not to feel
my porcelain dreams do not belong here
:
my paradise is adorned with golden gods
progressive sounds
your beauty
and mine
mystical beasts meditate on mescaline
all of you have become all of me
:
beyond, a new world awaits
the universe calls me by my name
before i'm ready
i dive
my first vision is of a child

noise

societal trials second guessing my sanity
staring at me like i am a side storm
far away from the norm
sugarcoating their realities
too scared to dwell on alternative scenes
sliding doors since high school
i try to squeeze in but i don't fit
i never will
space is only noise i suppose
:
spiritual surplus on the artist's behalf
living for the seconds that forever feel like the moment
of their occurrence
skip societal nonsense
space is only noise if you impose

modern spree

form dictates feeling
state of the art appliances for home improvements
stainless steel mirrored window films delivered to you
$20.27 a piece
for privacy from thy neighbor
(add to cart)
satellite images uncover those who actively question the rules
for our protection
the truth leaks
candid and clear
no one speaks
(add to cart)
previously political stencil art now on show with urban apparel
for the modern soul
(add to cart)
pyrite stones half off in stores displayed on vintage covers of 'Ham on Rye'
(add to cart)

the taste of love

a week has passed
in the dark, damp room
of the living
in my tent
:
under the spray painted commemoration
of them versus us
i fill the gaps of light with my torch
transcending language
awkwardly waiting for foreign aid to salvage my youth
we don't speak the same language
they are urban animals, their feet on city soil
and we are wild ones
caged in camps like the current forgot to take us
back
:
tomorrow i will be charged for stone throwing
what will the court of occupation say?
:
the taste of love is far from here
and if justice isn't served
we will serve it

those too

i found refuge in skin colors different than my own
an immigrant in my own home
i do not belong where i belong
can't you see?
we're the same
you and me
flat iron shirts and designer sleeves
well-groomed sins beneath your skin
underneath it all lies a heart so thin
:
how lucky it must have been to be you, white ben
you've tasted flavors of continents and seen the world
with your white eyes
i see dots on maps of places you have yet to visit
i envy you for your riches
but as i write this
i know your world bleeds through my pen too

the morning after

under the influence
of nothing
of everything
bare naked 40 calories per 25 ml
we drank out of bottles thinking it wouldn't count
math to us was doubt
art to us was fact
life to us was lived
us to us, bliss
still is
prerequisite curiosities or accidental exposures?
either way there are no closures
for once a mind is open
it is open

freetown

i'm elsewhere
the west side of it
politically correct *developing world*
coined by faces who conditioned it
digging precious stones on its behalf
:
i'm riding front seat
soaking up its heat with a sweet stranger
driving me to the rented room
that once held an abstracted vision
of what we could've been
:
i had dreams of becoming a painter
selling my shit online
i can see why you left me
but at the time twenty-one and vain felt so divine
:
the first chapter of our pain wasn't our last
if i could translate the love i had for you in forty-two languages
i would
but we're still driving
almost there but you're not here
i feel removed from the situation that is my life
i roll down the window
the wind is charged with odors of palm oil and sea water
there will be no panic attacks in paradise

key rose

can you hear the sirens?
soft metal barriers
there is no final destination but we are almost there
close enough to feel it
far enough to seek it
deep down dazed but not confused
he looks down
lends his key to a charcoal rose
and proceeds to produce
a form of life abuse
can't live with it
can't live without it
sounds in process
hearts in progress
all of a sudden
out of the desert's hue
nothing really happens
but everything has changed

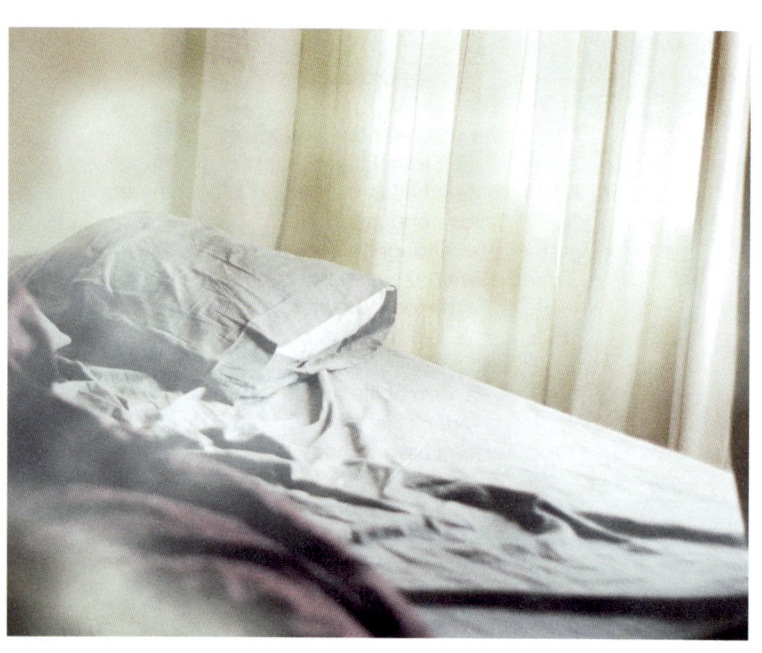

float

it's the butterfly from my bedsheets
full blown and flying in front of me
queen alexandra birdwing butterfly
hovering over the bedsheets that hosted her
closer
she dances above my nose in circular motions
her wings, a splash of color caught in a whirlwind
faster
spinning and dipping like a drunk in the sky
she stops
midair
marvelous
her large wings fold and release in slow motion
she's being considerate with her beauty
if only she could see herself
how she travels through space and time
sharing her youth with the world
and with me

inherited madness

wild at heart
not me
i trust my heart blind
it is my mind that is not mine
wide at heart
wild at mind
that's me
for all the ones i once loved
will continue to feel the delusion of my intensity
long-lived denials
short-lived trials
of a love that was their own
to a love that is now mine

a room outside

soon
but we'll fly away
i know
you don't want to be here
in the wild
butterfly that wouldn't last a minute
bear with me
:
behind
if you could leave these bed sheets